GLORIA

Children's Books

Nihil Obstat, Arthur J. Scanlan, S.T.D., Censor Liborum
Imprimatur ✠ Francis Cardinal Spellman,
Archbishop of New York
Cum Permissu Superiorum

William J. Hirten Co., Cumberland, RI

GLORIA
Children's Books

The Guardian Angels

Our Protectors

by Daniel A. Lord, S.J.

The Guardian Angels

Once upon a time,
all the angels in Heaven were good.
God had made them because
He loved them.
He had made them strong and beautiful.
But some of the angels were wicked.
They said, "Let us fight against God,
we will not obey Him."
The rest said, "That is bad. We love God.
He is our good Father.
We will do as He asks."

So there was a terrible fight in Heaven.
The bad angels tried to drive God out.
The good angels fought to protect Him.
The good angels won.
The bad angels were driven out of Heaven.
God thanked His good angels
and made them stronger
and more beautiful than ever.

Then God said,
"We will make men and women.
They will also be our children."
So He made a
son called Adam.
He made a beautiful
daughter named Eve.
They will live in Paradise and
be very happy.
Some day God wants to bring them
to Heaven with Him.
But one of the bad angels crawled up out of
Hell where he lived.
He hated Adam and Eve
because God loved them so much.

9

The evil angel lied to Adam and Eve
and they sinned.
God was sorry. But He saw that men
and women were going to have
strong enemies, the evil angels.
So He said;
"I will give them strong friends too.
I will give them good angels
to be with them always."
Whenever, then, God makes
another son or daughter,
He calls a good angel.
"Go to earth," He commands.
"Take care of my child.
You are a Guardian Angel."

So whenever babies are born,
down from Heaven come the angels.
Nobody can see them.
But they are strong and good
and beautiful.
They love that new baby very much.
They will try hard not to let
anything happen to the child.
From that time on, a Guardian Angel
never leaves his little friend.

They stay watching over
your cradle.
They are with you when you take
your first steps.
They are very happy on the day you make
your First Communion
They are watching over you
whenever you are at home, school or
playing sports by yourself or with others.
They help you to pray.
All through life they will be at the side
of that little child of God.

Sometimes boys and girls love
their Guardian Angels very much.
They talk to them and ask them for help.
Sometimes boys and girls
pay no attention to their
Guardian Angels.
But always your
Guardian Angel remains.
They are a friend and guide and
protector for life.

The Guardian Angels
know how sad it is to sin.
They know that sin made the bad angels
leave Heaven and turn into devils.
They know that sin spoils
the soul of a boy or girl.
So if a boy or girl sins,
the Guardian Angels are very sad.
When they see temptation coming close
to a boy or girl, they try to drive it away.
If a bad angel comes near, they
protect their little friend.

The boy and girl who listen
to their Guardian Angel will always be safe.
No evil angel can hurt them.
Their lives will be wonderfully happy.
Your Guardian Angel is with you all the time
so they can see everything you do.
They go with you every place you go.
They hear everything you say.
They are very happy when they see you do
things that are good. They are delighted
when you speak in friendly ways.
They smile at you
when you are kind to your parents.

21

But can't you see how sad they are
when you do things that are bad.
They wish you never would do
anything bad.
They don't like to hear you speak in any way
that is not sweet and pure and good.
Don't you want to make your
Guardian Angel always proud of you?
Don't you want them to be glad that you
are their little friend?

If a person is good, death is very lovely.
It is just the dark gate through which
we walk into Heaven.
It is the beginning of joy
that never ends.
When we come to die,
our Guardian Angel will be at our bedside.
They will frighten away the evil angels
who want to hurt us.
They will whisper into our ear prayers
that we can say.

They will remind God
of all the good we have done.
They will help us to be sorry
for any evil we did.
They will take us by the hand
and lead us to God.
We will not be afraid.
We will walk to the gate of Heaven
with an angel at our side.
Our Guardian Angel
will lead us safely to Jesus.

Angel of God,
My Guardian Dear,
to whom His love commits me here;
Ever this day (or night) be at my side,
to light and guard, to rule and guide.